More
than

Sparrows

Vi Fansler

Other books by Vi Fansler:
MORE THAN BLACKBERRIES 1979 *(out of print)*
MORE THAN A SCARECROW 1982 *(out of print)*

DEDICATION OF THE BOOK

My family's love, encouragement and assistance in whatever I do has made my journey a joyful one! I dedicate this book to each of them, whom I dearly love with all my heart:

To Bob, my wonderful husband and closest friend for over 47 years.
To our dear children and dear grandchildren:
       Jim & Angie Fansler, Drew, Brian and Libby
       Debi & Dennie Doud, Brennan and Aubree
       Jerry & Mary Fansler, Joshua, Jason, Megan and Jonathan
       Dave & Dawn Fansler
   and to three dear grandchildren
       who went to be with Jesus before they were born.

The Apostle John wrote: *It gave me great joy to have some brothers come and tell about your faithfulness to the truth and how you continue to walk in the truth. I have no greater joy than to hear that my children are walking in the truth.* – from III John 3-4

Dear Lord:
I would say, *"Me, too!"*
I have no greater joy than to hear
that my children and grandchildren
are walking with You –
every child and every grandchild
loving You,
obeying You,
knowing You
whom to know is eternal life.

There is no greater joy for me!

And, Lord,
I hear You saying,
"Me, too!"

CONTENTS BY TITLE

(Note: For Scripture references,   pages are arranged Genesis through Revelation.)

In the beginning God created the heavens and the earth. And God said, "Let the land produce vegetation. Let the water teem with living creatures, and let birds fly above the earth across the expanse of the sky. Let the land produce living creatures – livestock, creatures that move along the ground, and wild animals. Let us make man in our image, in our likeness." And the Lord God formed man from the dust of the ground and breathed into his nostrils the breath of life, and man became a living being. Then the Lord God made a woman from the rib He had taken out of the man, and He brought her to the man. – from Genesis 1:1-26 & 2:7,22

Dear Creator God:

You created everything else first –
the land, sky, sea, vegetation,
the sun, moon, stars,
animals, fish and birds – including many sparrows.
Then You formed a man.
Finally You created a woman.

Did You create her last because
You knew that if You created her first,
she would have lots of advice
about where to place the stars,
what shape to make the moon,
and which way the stripes should go on the zebra?

Or was it that You wanted the woman
to be Your grand finale?
Or was it just that You knew how much
she liked apples?

_____

Joseph had a dream, and when he told it to his brothers, they hated him all the more. His brothers said to him, "Do you intend to reign over us? Will you actually rule us?" And they hated him all the more because of his dream and what he had said. – from Genesis 37:5 & 8

Dear God:

In the Old Testament
Joseph was loved by his father
more than anyone can imagine –
and hated by his brothers *all the more!*

In the New Testament
Jesus was loved by You, His Father,
more than anyone can imagine –
and hated by His brothers *all the more!*

Sometimes it's difficult to put it all together!

But You do!
The hatred of Joseph became the means
of salvation for the ones who did the hating!

The crucifixion of Jesus became the means
of salvation for the ones who did the crucifying!

You, God,
put it all together!

When the news reached Pharaoh's palace that Joseph's brothers had come, Pharaoh and all his officials were pleased. Pharaoh said to Joseph, "Tell your brothers, 'Do this: load your animals and return to the land of Canaan, and bring your father and your families back to me.'" Joseph gave them carts, as Pharaoh had commanded, and he also gave them provisions for their journey. Then he sent his brothers away, and as they were leaving he said to them, "Don't quarrel on the way!" – from Genesis 45:16-24

Dear Lord Jesus:

Do I hear You say to me and my spiritual siblings,
as Joseph said to his brothers,
"Don't quarrel on the way?"

Along life's journey
we have quarreled about
many *important* things
such as
the color of the carpet in the sanctuary,
how plush to make the pads on the pews,
what size and shape of cross,
about the style of music!
Especially the style of music!

Lord,
as we go about our
discussing,
bickering,
squabbling,
caterwauling –
may we remember the words:
"Don't quarrel on the way!"

But the more the Israelites were oppressed, the more they multiplied and spread. – from Exodus 1:12

Dear Lord God:

In the days of long ago,
the rulers of Egypt
attempted
to *subtract*
the number of Hebrews
by oppressing them
and destroying their newborn.

In these days,
the rulers of darkness
attempt
to *divide*
the number of believers
by depressing them
and destroying their newborn.

But You,
Lord God,
are more than able
to *add*
and *multiply*
when evil men try to
subtract
and *divide!*

That's a real *plus!*

Then the Lord said to Moses, "Go to Pharaoh and say to him, 'This is what the Lord says: Let my people go, so that they may worship me. If you refuse to let them go, I will plague your whole country with frogs. The Nile will teem with frogs. They will come up into your palace and your bedroom and onto your bed, into the houses of your officials and on your people, and into your ovens and kneading troughs. The frogs will go up on you and your people and all your officials.'" So Aaron stretched out his hand over the waters of Egypt, and the frogs came up and covered the land. But the magicians did the same things by their secret arts; they also made frogs come up on the land of Egypt. – from Exodus 8:1-6

Dear Lord:

When You sent the plague of frogs on Egypt,
and everything and everyone
was covered with frogs,
it seems incredible
that Pharaoh asked his magicians
to produce *more* frogs!

Then with frogs everywhere,
Pharaoh asked Moses to pray
that You would take away the frogs
tomorrow!

Why not *today? Right now?*

I think *one* more night
with frogs in *my* bed,
and I would have croaked!

The Lord said to Moses and Aaron in Egypt, "This month is to be for you the first month, the first month of your year. Tell the whole community of Israel that on the tenth day of this month each man is to take a lamb for his family, one for each household. Take care of them until the fourteenth day of the month, when all the people of the community of Israel must slaughter them at twilight. Then they are to take some of the blood and put it on the sides and tops of the doorframes of the houses where they eat the lambs. This is how you are to eat it: with your cloak tucked into your belt, your sandals on your feet and your staff in your hand. Eat it in haste; it is the Lord's Passover." – from Exodus 12:1-11

Dear Lord:

When the Israelites ate the Passover,
they were ready for a journey.

They wore their traveling clothes
and hiking shoes,
and they had walking sticks in their hands.

They didn't dally over the Passover Supper.

I wonder, as I partake of the Lord's Supper,
am I prepared to travel?
Am I packed up,
ready to go wherever You want me to go?
Or do I dilly-dally in my lounging robe,
barefoot and empty-handed,
without a thought about going anywhere?

Lord,
I want to be suited, shod and staffed
for Your next supper!

Then Moses went up to God, and the Lord called to him from the mountain and said, "This is what you are to say to the house of Jacob and what you are to tell the people of Israel: 'You yourselves have seen what I did to Egypt, and how I carried you on eagles' wings and brought you to Myself. Now if you obey Me fully and keep My covenant, then out of all nations you will be My treasured possession.'" – from Exodus 19:3-5

Dear God:

You said that You carry
those You love
on the
wings of eagles.

God,
that would take some *very* large eagles!

But then,
You created a *very* large fish
to swallow Jonah!

So then,
You can create an eagle
big enough
to carry me!

A CLOUD OR FIRE?

When Moses went up on the mountain, the cloud covered it, and the glory of the Lord settled on Mount Sinai. For six days the cloud covered the mountain, and on the seventh day the Lord called to Moses from within the cloud. To the Israelites the glory of the Lord looked like a consuming fire on top of the mountain. – from Exodus 24:15-17

Dear Lord:

When Moses was on the mountain,
Your glory was like a cloud,
but to the Israelites far below
Your glory was like a fire!

The difference
was the distance.

When I am close to You,
You are like a comforting cloud.

When I am far away from Your presence,
You are like a frightening fire.

Lord God,
I would rather climb the mountain
and see You in the cloud –
than view You from the valley!

I'm putting on my climbing gear!

The Lord instructed Moses regarding peace offerings: *"If his offering is a goat, he is to present it before the Lord. He is to lay his hand on its head and slaughter it in front of the Tent of Meeting. Then Aaron's sons shall sprinkle its blood against the altar on all sides. From what he offers he is to make this offering to the Lord by fire: all the fat that covers the inner parts or is connected to them, both kidneys with the fat on them near the loins, and the covering of the liver, which he will remove with the kidneys. The priest shall burn them on the altar as food, an offering made by fire, a pleasing aroma. All the fat is the Lord's."* – from Leviticus 3:12-16

Dear Lord God:

In the Old Testament
when offerings of animals were made,
You said all the fat was Yours.

I no longer make atonement
with a sheep or goat,
since Your Son died for me.

But I wonder, Lord God,
is all the fat still Yours?

I gladly give You
all of mine!

The Lord said to Moses, *"If he cannot afford a lamb, he is to bring two doves or two young pigeons to the Lord as a penalty for his sin – one for a sin offering and the other for a burnt offering. He is to bring them to the priest, who shall first offer the one for the sin offering. He is to wring its head from its neck, not severing it completely, and is to sprinkle some of the blood of the sin offering against the side of the altar; the rest of the blood must be drained out at the base of the altar. It is a sin offering."* – from Leviticus 5:7-9

Dear Lord God:

In the Old Testament,
a person who couldn't afford a lamb
as a sin offering
could give two doves or pigeons.

In the case of a bird,
the priest would wring its neck
before putting it on the altar.

I wonder
if some people back then
gave a bird
when they could have afforded
a lamb?

Lord God,
how often do You feel like
wringing the neck
of *my* offering?

Then Moses said to Aaron, "Take your censer and put incense in it, along with fire from the altar, and hurry to the assembly to make atonement for them. Wrath has come out from the Lord; the plague has started." So Aaron did as Moses said, and ran into the midst of the assembly. The plague had already started among the people, but Aaron offered the incense and made atonement for them. He stood between the living and the dead, and the plague stopped. – from Numbers 16:46-48

Dear Lord Jesus:

In the desert of Sinai,
Aaron stood
between the living and the dead.

He made atonement for the Israelites
so the sickness would cease
and people would not die.

Aaron made an *earthly* difference!

On the hill of Calvary
You hung
between the living and the dead.

You made atonement for the whole world
so that sin could cease
and people would never die.

You, Lord Jesus, made an *eternal* difference!

Moses said: *"These are the commandments the Lord proclaimed in a loud voice to your whole assembly there on the mountain from out of the fire, the cloud and the deep darkness; and He added nothing more. Then He wrote them on two stone tablets and gave them to me."* Jesus said, *"You have heard that it was said to the people long ago, 'Do not murder, and anyone who murders will be subject to judgment.' But I tell you that anyone who is angry with his brother will be subject to judgment. You have heard that it was said, 'Do not commit adultery.' But I tell you that anyone who looks at a woman lustfully has already committed adultery with her in his heart. You have heard it said, 'Love your neighbor and hate your enemy.' But I tell you: Love your enemies, and pray for those who persecute you."* – from Deuteronomy 5:22 & Matthew 5:21-44

Dear Father God:

When You gave the Ten Commandments to Moses
You *added* nothing more.

Then Your Son Jesus *summed* it up:
To *"Do not murder"* He added, *"Do not be angry."*
To *"Do not commit adultery"* He added, *"Do not lust."*
To *"Love your neighbor"* He added, *"Love your enemies."*

Now there's nothing more to be added.

Forgive me for adding something more for others to obey,
filling in the blanks to fit *my* own ideas:

Do not _____.
Do not _____.
Do not _____.
Do not _____.

Lord, why do I *add* something more –
as if *my* rules are the last word?

Your Word is always the last word!

You may say to yourselves, "These nations are stronger than we are. How can we drive them out?" But do not be afraid of them; remember well what the Lord your God did to Pharaoh and to all Egypt. You saw with your own eyes the great trials, the miraculous signs and wonders, the mighty hand and outstretched arm, with which the Lord your God brought you out. The Lord your God will do the same to all the peoples you now fear. Do not be terrified by them, for the Lord your God, who is among you, is a great and awesome God.
– from Deuteronomy 7:17-21

Dear Lord my God:

May I not look at the size or strength
of my enemy –
even out of the corner of my eye!

Instead,
may I fix my eye on You,
my great and awesome God!

Instead of the girth of Goliath,
may I see the muscle of my Maker!

Instead of the strength of Satan,
may I see the dynamics of the Divine!

Lord God,
guard even the corner of my eye!

God instructed Moses: You may eat any clean bird. *But these you*
may not eat: the eagle, the vulture, the black vulture, the red kite, the
black kite, any kind of falcon, any kind of raven, the horned owl, the
screech owl, the gull, any kind of hawk, the little owl, the great owl,
the white owl, the desert owl, the osprey, the cormorant, the stork,
any kind of heron, the hoopoe and the bat. – from Deuteronomy
14:11-18

Dear Lord God:

When the rules were written back in the days of Moses,
some birds were labeled clean
and other birds unclean.

The clean could be eaten,
and the unclean could not.

What made some birds
dirty birds?

What made the difference?
I really don't know.

But what *I* need to be concerned about is this:
Is *this* old bird
clean
or unclean?

And I know what makes the difference!

It is the blood of Jesus!

Then the Lord said to Joshua, "See, I have delivered Jericho into your hands, along with its king and its fighting men. March around the city once with all the armed men. Do this for six days. Have seven priests carry trumpets of rams' horns in front of the ark. On the seventh day, march around the city seven times, with the priests blowing the trumpets. When you hear them sound a long blast on the trumpets, have all the people give a loud shout; then the wall of the city will collapse and the people will go up, every man straight in." –
from Joshua 6:2-5

Dear Lord:

If I were Joshua, I may have questioned Your battle plan.

I might have said,
"You want me to do WHAT?
You want the clergy and the army
to march in absolute silence
around the walled city of Jericho
for six days –
And then on the seventh day
to march seven times
and then blow trumpets and shout?"

But Joshua didn't question You
and the walls of Jericho came tumbling down!

Lord,
forgive me for questioning Your orders,
for asking,
"You want me to do WHAT?"

I have some walls that need to come down.

Samson awoke from his sleep and thought, "I'll go out as before and shake myself free." But he did not know that the Lord had left him. – from Judges 16:20

Dear Lord:

Samson didn't know that *You* had left him,
and he didn't know that without *You* He was nothing –
though he had been sanctified from birth
and his parents had been tutored by an angel
on how to raise him.

You gave Samson incredible physical strength!
With his bare hands, he killed a lion.
He struck down thirty Philistines.
He caught three hundred foxes
and tied them tail to tail in pairs.
He broke ropes as if they were string.
He killed a thousand men with the jawbone of a donkey.
He tore loose the doors of the city gate
and carried them to the top of the hill.

No animal or army could defeat him,
no rope or city gate could hold him –
until he fell asleep in the wrong arms!

Then the Philistines blinded him and bound him
and put him to work grinding their grain.

God, may *I* never forget that without *You* I am nothing,
no matter how sanctified or schooled.
May I remember that sin blinds and binds and grinds
and the only safe place to fall asleep
is in *Your* arms!

Now in earlier times in Israel, for the redemption and transfer of property to become final, one party took off his sandal and gave it to the other. This was the method of legalizing transactions in Israel. – from Ruth 4:7

Dear Lord God:

There was a custom in ancient Bethlehem
that when a person transferred ownership of property,
he would take off his sandal
and give it to the buyer –
implying he no longer had the right
to walk on that property.

Instead of turning over keys
to the new owner,
the seller turned over his sandal!

Lord God,
You bought me with Your Son's blood –
but I doubt that all the property has been transferred.

Here's my sandal, Lord!

Both of them!

But the Lord said to Samuel, "Do not consider his appearance or his height, for I have rejected him. The Lord does not look at the things man looks at. Man looks at the outward appearance, but the Lord looks at the heart." – from I Samuel 16:7

Dear God:

You often choose the most unlikely people.

The prophet Samuel was to anoint the next king of Israel
from among the eight sons of Jesse.
Samuel thought You would choose Eliab
who was the eldest and tallest and most kingly looking.
But You said,
"No!"

Then before Samuel passed six more sons of Jesse,
not quite as tall or kingly -
and You said,
"No! No! No! No! No! No!"

So from the fields Jesse called in one more son:
his youngest,
probably his shortest and most unprincely son –
a shepherd boy named David.
And You shouted,
"YES!"

You often choose the most unlikely in *our* eyes.
With *Your* eyes
You can see the heart!

Jonathan son of Saul had a son who was lame in both feet. He was five years old when the news about Saul and Jonathan came from Jezreel. His nurse picked him up and fled, but as she hurried to leave, he fell and became crippled. His name was Mephibosheth. – from II Samuel 4:4

Dear Lord God:

I like what happened *later* to Mephibosheth,
who as a child became crippled in both feet
through a fall.

When David became King,
he brought Mephibosheth to his palace,
and he ate at the king's table
as if he were one of the king's sons.

Dear Lord,
I like what happened *later* to me,
who as a child became crippled
through *the* fall.

Thank You, King Jesus, for inviting me
to eat at Your table
as one of Your children.

When I'm seated at Your table,
others cannot see my crippled feet –
nor can I see theirs!

EXCEPT

For David had done what was right in the eyes of the Lord and had not failed to keep any of the Lord's commands all the days of his life – except in the case of Uriah the Hittite. – from I Kings 15:5

Dear Lord:

King David obeyed fully – *except.*

He kept all Your commands
all the days of his life –
except!

David's *except*
was adultery with Bathsheba
and the murder of her husband Uriah.

Oh Lord,
if *my* disobedience and failure were recorded
for all to read,
what would You say
were my *excepts*?

Though my
*except*ions
may not include a Bathsheba or Uriah,
my sin is just as sinful.

Thank You, oh Lord,
for Your *exceptional* forgiveness!

Then the word of the Lord came to Elijah: "Leave here, turn eastward and hide in the Kerith Ravine, east of the Jordan. You will drink from the brook, and I have ordered the ravens to feed you there." So he did what the Lord had told him. He went to the Kerith Ravine, east of the Jordan, and stayed there. The ravens brought him bread and meat in the morning and bread and meat in the evening, and he drank from the brook. – from I Kings 17:2-6

Dear Lord:

Elijah
ate like a bird!
You ordered the ravens to feed him.

I doubt the ravens poked food in his mouth
as though Elijah were a baby bird!
Probably they dropped the bread
and meat *(not worms, I hope!)*
into his hand.

You could have chosen some other way
for Your prophet to get his food.
But You chose the birds.

Lord,
may I obey Your orders
when You choose
this old bird
to feed someone.

"Don't be afraid," the prophet answered. "Those who are with us are more than those who are with them." And Elisha prayed, "O Lord, open his eyes so he may see." Then the Lord opened the servant's eyes, and he looked and saw the hills full of horses and chariots of fire all around Elisha. – from II Kings 6:16-17

Dear God:

In any war, I want to be on *Your* side!

For though the enemy has armies of millions,
You, God,
are *more* than they!

I'd rather face the enemy
alone with *You*
than to have all the weapons
of all the earth
on my side!

May I keep this in mind the next time
guns fire,
swords rattle,
cannons shoot,
missiles fly,
and bombs explode!

You, Lord,
are my shield and shelter
and my sanctuary!

Now David was clothed in a robe of fine linen, as were all the Levites who were carrying the ark, and as were the singers, and Kenaniah, who was in charge of the singing of the choirs. David also wore a linen ephod. So all Israel brought up the ark of the covenant of the Lord with shouts, with the sounding of rams' horns and trumpets, and of cymbals, and the playing of lyres and harps. As the ark of the covenant of the Lord was entering the City of David, Michal daughter of Saul watched from a window. And when she saw King David dancing and celebrating, she despised him in her heart. – from I Chronicles 15:27-29

Dear Lord God:

What a celebration that must have been
when the Ark of the Covenant
was being returned to Jerusalem.

There were choirs singing,
people shouting,
horns blowing,
cymbals clanging,
harps playing,
and a king dancing.

The only one
who didn't like the style of worship
was Michal.

You, Lord God, enjoyed it!

May I join Your celebration –
no matter what the style!

Josiah was eight years old when he became king, and he reigned in Jerusalem thirty-one years. He did what was right in the eyes of the Lord and walked in the ways of his father David, not turning aside to the right or to the left. Zedekiah was twenty-one years old when he became king, and he reigned in Jerusalem eleven years. He did evil in the eyes of the Lord his God and did not humble himself. He became stiff-necked and hardened his heart and would not turn to the Lord, the God of Israel. The Lord, the God of their fathers, sent word to them through His messengers again and again, because He had pity on His people and on His dwelling place. But they mocked God's messengers, despised His words and scoffed at His prophets until the wrath of the Lord was aroused against His people and there was no remedy. Consider therefore the kindness and sternness of God: sternness to those who fell, but kindness to you, provided that you continue in His kindness. Otherwise, you also will be cut off. – from II Chronicles 34:1-2; 36:11-16 & Romans 11:22

Dear Lord God:

In the Old Testament, there were good kings
who did what was right in Your eyes.
They walked with You
and led their people up the right path.
You blessed them, prospered them,
protected them and fought for them.

Also there were bad kings who did evil in Your eyes.
They walked away from You
and led their people down the wrong path.
You withdrew Your blessing and they were destroyed.

Lord God,
may I consider both Your kindness and sternness.
May I never forget that when I refuse *Your* remedy,
there is no other remedy.

When the builders laid the foundation of the temple of the Lord, the priests in their vestments and with trumpets, and the Levites (the sons of Asaph) with cymbals, took their places to praise the Lord, as prescribed by David king of Israel. With praise and thanksgiving they sang to the Lord: "He is good; His love to Israel endures forever." And all the people gave a great shout of praise to the Lord, because the foundation of the house of the Lord was laid. But many of the older priests and Levites and family heads, who had seen the former temple, wept aloud when they saw the foundation of this temple being laid, while many others shouted for joy. No one could distinguish the sound of the shouts of joy from the sound of weeping, because the people made so much noise. And the sound was heard far away. – from Ezra 3:10-13

Dear Lord God:

How happy those Israelites must have been
when they saw the temple foundation laid!

Some played trumpets.
Some played cymbals.
Some sang.
All shouted.
Some wept for joy!
Some shouted for joy!

The celebration was heard far away.

Lord God,
in whatever way my praise is expressed,
I wonder if it can it be heard far away?

I hope *You* hear it!
But then, You are *not* far away!

MORE THAN A FOURTH OF A DAY

On the twenty-fourth day of the same month, the Israelites gathered together, fasting and wearing sackcloth and having dust on their heads. They stood in their places and confessed their sins and the wickedness of their fathers. They stood where they were and read from the Book of the Law of the Lord their God for a fourth of the day, and spent another fourth in confession and in worshipping the Lord their God. – from Nehemiah 9:1-3

Dear Lord my God:

I wonder if it would be well
if I did
a day of fasting,
wearing sackcloth and dust,
reading Your Book for a fourth of the day,
confessing my sins for a fourth of the day
and worshipping You.

Surely confession was not just for those
of Nehemiah's day –
unless
I think I have
no sin
to confess!

Oh, Lord God,
I'll need
more
than a fourth of a day!

And Mordecai answered Esther, "And who knows but that you have come to royal position for such a time as this?" Then Esther sent this reply to Mordecai: "Go, gather together all the Jews who are in Susa, and fast for me. Do not eat or drink for three days, night or day. I and my maids will fast as you do. When this is done, I will go to the king, even though it is against the law. And if I perish, I perish." – from Esther 4:14-16

Dear Lord God:

I would like to be as courageous as Esther!

The king could have taken her life,
when she went to see him
without being summoned.

Yet she *wasn't* foolhardy.
She had fasted and prayed
before she took action.

Often with a harebrained plan up my sleeve,
I rush into action –
and only later,
when my strategy doesn't solve the problem,
do I think about
fasting and prayer.

Lord God,
help me to put my *action cart*
behind the *horse*
of fasting and prayer!

May I remember there's no power in my cart!

*In the land of Uz there lived a man whose name was Job. This man
was blameless and upright; he feared God and shunned evil. He had
seven sons and three daughters, and he owned 7,000 sheep, 3,000
camels, 500 yoke of oxen and 500 donkeys, and had a large number of
servants. He was the greatest man among all the people of the East.
His sons used to take turns holding feasts in their homes, and they
would invite their three sisters to eat and drink with them. When a
period of feasting had run its course, Job would send and have them
purified. Early in the morning he would sacrifice a burnt offering for
each of them, thinking, "Perhaps my children have sinned and cursed
God in their hearts." This was Job's regular custom.* – from Job
1:1-5

Dear God:

I've read about this man called Job.
He was a righteous, family man.

His *regular* practice was
to call his grown children together
so that he might have them purified,
offering a sacrifice
for each of them.

What a scene that must have been –
Job's ten children with their families
coming together around Your altar!

Dear God,
there's one better scene
than to have all my family around *my* supper table –
and that's to have all of them
around *Yours!*

BIRDS, CRICKETS, LOCUSTS, FROGS & KATYDIDS

The grasslands of the desert overflow; the hills are clothed with gladness. The meadows are covered with flocks and the valleys are mantled with grain; they shout for joy and sing. – from Psalm 65:12-13

Dear Lord:

Today I heard a hill laugh
and a grassland shout for joy.

I heard a meadow sing
and a valley shout Your Name!

The birds, crickets, locusts, frogs and katydids
all had a melody for You.

Nature's chorus is music to Your ears!

Lord,
I want to join the choir!

I want my praise to You
to be as persistent
as that of the cricket, locust and katydid!

And though my voice
will never sound like a canary's –
surely I can do as well as the frog!

Lord,
may I croak Your praise
until I croak!

Praise be to the Lord, to God our Savior, who daily bears our burdens. – from Psalm 68:19

Dear God my Savior:

Thank You for
daily
unloading my burdens.

I'm glad I don't have to wait
until next year
or next month,
or next week,
or even tomorrow
to have You take them.

As each burden comes,
You lift it!

That way they don't pile up
on my conveyor belt –
unless in some foolish moment I tell You
that I can handle this day all by myself!

Lord,
why in the world
would I do that?

Even the sparrow has found a home, and the swallow a nest for herself, where she may have her young – a place near Your altar, O Lord Almighty, my King and my God. Blessed are those who dwell in Your house; they are ever praising You. – from Psalm 84:3-4

Dear Lord:

Like the sparrow
and the swallow in the Psalm,
let me build my home
near Your altar.

What a home site!

Those little birds were bright!

They sang Your praises
as they carefully built their nests
near to You
to raise their young.

Oh Lord,
may
this big bird
be as smart as
those little birds!

For the Lord is good and His love endures forever; His faithfulness
continues through all generations. – from Psalm 100:5

Dear Lord:

Thank You for Your kind of love!
It's good,
faithful,
pure,
enduring
and secure.

I know I can trust You, Lord, with my heart.

You love with an everlasting love!

You will never, ever,
down the road,
say,
"I didn't mean it!"

You will never, ever,
down the road
say,
"I've changed My mind!"

Thank You
for Your *forever* kind of love!

Hear my prayer, O Lord; let my cry for help come to You. Do not hide Your face from me when I am in distress. Turn Your ear to me; when I call, answer me quickly. I am like a desert owl, like an owl among ruins. I lie awake; I have become like a bird alone on a housetop. – from Psalm 102:1-7

Dear Lord:

At times I feel like a bird
alone
on a housetop!

For reasons of their own,
all the other birds have flown away!
If birds of a feather flock together,
I must be an odd bird
with peculiar feathers.

Then, Lord,
I realize You're there on the housetop
with *this* lonely bird –
and You tell me You will never leave me.

Then You ask,
*"But why are you sitting here on the housetop
when you can fly?"*

Oh, Lord! I had forgotten that I could fly!

How wonderful to feel
Your wind beneath my wings!

The birds of the air nest by the waters; they sing among the branches.
He waters the mountains from His upper chambers; the earth is
satisfied by the fruit of His work. He makes grass grow for the cattle,
and plants for man to cultivate – bringing forth food from the earth:
wine that gladdens the heart of man, oil to make his face shine, and
bread that sustains his heart.   – from Psalm 104:12-15

Dear Lord:

Do I act as if praise
is only for the birds?

They sing Your praises
each and every day
as they perch on the branches of the trees.

Lord,
today *this* big old bird
is building her nest
close to the Living Water –
and from my perch
I will praise You!

And, Lord,
may my praise to You
enable *this* bird in Your hand
to win two in the bush!

The trees of the Lord are well watered, the cedars of Lebanon that He planted. There the birds make their nests; the stork has its home in the pine trees. – from Psalm 104:16-17

Dear Lord:

You provide a place for the birds to make their nests
and You make sure they have something to eat.

I try to assist You, Lord,
by keeping the bird feeders filled.

But today
some birds were hopping around on the ground
beneath the feeder,
scratching for a few spilled seeds,
while a few feet above them
there was an abundant supply.

Lord,
how often am I like the birds?

You have an abundant supply
if I fly a little higher –
but I stay on the ground,
scratching around in the dirt –
when all the while,
if I look up
and try my wings,
You have the feeder full!

OFFENSES _____

A man's wisdom gives him patience; it is to his glory to overlook an offense. – from Proverbs 19:11

Dear Lord:

You say it is to my glory to
overlook
an offense.

Well, today I'm *in*glorious!

I failed to overlook a wrong.

Instead,
I looked it over
and over
and over
and over
and it didn't look any better in the end
than it did at first!

Lord,
help me
to overlook!

That has to be done only once –
for to overlook
is to forgive
and never
look it over again!

Cast but a glance at riches, and they are gone, for they will surely sprout wings and fly off to the sky like an eagle. – from Proverbs 23:5

Dear Lord:

If the sweepstakes bird
ever lands in my yard,
I would like to clip its wings
before it flies away!

Yet I know in my heart
that this world's riches
won't last long!

That's why I should
give only a *brief* glance
at wealth,
if I ever see it at all –

but take a *long* look
at You,
Everlasting Lord!

Do not revile the king even in your thoughts – because a bird of the air may carry your words, and a bird on the wing may report what you say. – from Ecclesiastes 10:20

Dear God my King:

Did a little bird tell You?

Someone reported to You what I said –
even what I thought!

Every private muttering
You seem to know.

At the baptism of Jesus,
the Holy Spirit descended
in the form of a dove.

Is that the Bird that told You, God?

Help me to speak wise words
and think pure thoughts.

Then I'll never have to be a fearful bird watcher!

Then I can enjoy the presence
of Your Holy Dove.

Remember your Creator in the days of your youth, before the days of trouble come and the years approach when you will say, "I find no pleasure in them" - before the sun and the light and the moon and the stars grow dark, and the clouds return after the rain; when the keepers of the house tremble, and the strong men stoop, when the grinders cease because they are few, and those looking through the windows grow dim; when the doors to the street are closed and the sound of grinding fades; when men rise up at the sound of birds, but all their songs grow faint; when men are afraid of heights and of dangers in the streets; when the almond tree blossoms and the grasshopper drags himself along and desire no longer is stirred. Then man goes to his eternal home and mourners go about the streets. Remember Him - before the silver cord is severed, or the golden bowl is broken; before the pitcher is shattered at the spring, or the wheel broken at the well, and the dust returns to the ground it came from, and the spirit returns to God who gave it. - from Ecclesiastes 12:1-7

Dear Lord God:

I pray that every one of my children and grandchildren
will remember You in the days of their youth -
before old age comes -
before their hands tremble
and their legs grow weak -
before their teeth are few
and their eyes dim and their ears dull -
before they cannot sleep and they get up with the birds!

God, may they remember You
before their hair turns white -
before their minds are unclear -
before their hearts fail and death comes.

Oh God, may they not be able to forget You!

Place me like a seal over your heart, like a seal over your arm; for love is as strong as death, its jealousy unyielding as the grave. It burns like blazing fire, like a mighty flame. Many waters cannot quench love; rivers cannot wash it away. If one were to give all the wealth of his house for love, it would be utterly scorned. – from Song of Songs 8:6-7

Dear Lord Jesus:

True love is a rare bird –
stronger than death,
defying the grave.

Among faith, hope and love,
love is the greatest.

It's priceless!
It cannot be bought or sold.

Lord,
if one person loves another
with true love,
he would die for the other,
if *need* be!

And Lord Jesus,
You *needed* to die for me.

*The Lord said to me, "Take a large scroll and write on it with an
ordinary pen."* - from Isaiah 8:1

Dear Lord God:

On one of my journeys far from home,
I sat down to read Your Word.
I looked for my *special* pen
with which to make notes in the margins of my Bible.

It was a *special* pen.
It didn't bleed through or smudge the pages.

But it couldn't be found anywhere,
though I searched pockets and purses,
suits and suitcases,
cubbyholes and closets.

Lord, You must have chuckled
as You watched me
raking the room for that *special* pen!

You knew that on that particular morning
when I finally sat down with an *ordinary* pen,
I would begin reading from Isaiah, chapter 8, verse 1:

*"Take a large scroll
and write on it with an ordinary pen!"*

Lord, did You laugh?
I did!

Even the stork in the sky knows her appointed seasons, and the dove, the swift and the thrush observe the time of their migration. But my people do not know the requirements of the Lord. – from Jeremiah 8:7

Dear Lord:

Sometimes I wish I were a bird!

Birds seem to know
instinctively
the time and place
You have planned for them to migrate.

They take off on schedule
and arrive at the appointed place.

Lord,
I have asked You,
*"What should I do? Where should I go?
When should I leave? When should I arrive?"*

I sit on my perch, not going anywhere.

Somehow I've missed Your signal.

Lord,
tell me again.

At Your direction, I'll fly the coop!

So Jeremiah the prophet said to all the people of Judah and to all those living in Jerusalem: For twenty-three years - from the thirteenth year of Josiah son of Amon king of Judah until this very day - the word of the Lord has come to me and I have spoken to you again and again, but you have not listened. And though the Lord has sent you all His servants and prophets again and again, you have not listened or paid any attention. - from Jeremiah 25:2-4

Dear Lord God:

Was Jeremiah discouraged?

He had preached to his people
for 23 years,
and for 23 years
they did not listen or pay attention!

Every sermon went down the drain!

He probably was hoping You would send him
to pastor another parish -
for these folks were *not* listening
big time!

Dear God,
are sermons still going down the drain?

Oh, may I pay attention and listen
big time -
so I may be ready for
Your big time!

*Because of the Lord's great love we are not consumed, for His
compassions never fail. They are new every morning; great is Your
faithfulness. I say to myself, "The Lord is my portion; therefore I will
wait for Him." The Lord is good to those whose hope is in Him, to
the one who seeks Him; it is good to wait quietly for the salvation of
the Lord.*   – from Lamentations 3:22-26

Dear Lord:

I am so glad
Your love cannot fail.

I am so glad
Your mercies are never stale!

They are new every morning when they arrive!

Lord,
as I wait for my inheritance,
may I do it quietly –
without complaining and murmuring
about the size of my portion –

for *You*,
Lord God,
are my inheritance!

What a legacy of love and mercy!

This is what the Sovereign Lord says: Woe to the shepherds of Israel who only take care of themselves! Should not shepherds take care of the flock? You have not strengthened the weak or healed the sick or bound up the injured. You have not brought back the strays or searched for the lost. You have ruled them harshly and brutally. As for you, My flock, this is what the Sovereign Lord says: I will judge between one sheep and another. Is it not enough for you to feed on the good pasture? Must you also trample the rest of your pasture with your feet? Is it not enough for you to drink clear water? Must you also muddy the rest with your feet? Must My flock feed on what you have trampled and drink what you have muddied with your feet? Because you shove with flank and shoulder, butting all the weak sheep with your horns until you have driven them away, I will save My flock, and they will no longer be plundered. I will judge between one sheep and another. – from Ezekiel 34:2-22

Dear Sovereign Lord:

I'm *not* a shepherd –
but if I were I would take seriously Your warning.

You said *"Woe"* to the shepherds
who think only of themselves,
who don't care about weak, sick, injured or lost sheep.

Then You warn the sheep – and I take that seriously!
I *am* one of them!

You said *"Woe"* to the sheep who stomp the pasture
and muddy the water and shove with their shoulder
and butt with their horns!

Lord, I hope on *this* old sheep
You don't see green and muddy feet
or an oversized shoulder!
And about the butting, Lord –
remove my horns!

But at that time your people – everyone whose name is found written in the book – will be delivered. Multitudes who sleep in the dust of the earth will awake: some to everlasting life, others to shame and everlasting contempt. Those who are wise will shine like the brightness of the heavens, and those who lead many to righteousness, like the stars for ever and ever. – from Daniel 12:1-3

Dear Lord God:

What a time that will be
when Your book is opened
and the names are read
and the graves are opened
and the dead come forth.

What a time that will be
when those who have received Your salvation
will shine as bright lights in the heavens
and those who have led others to You
will shine as stars.

But, Lord, for some the scene on that night
will not be bright and light
when Your book is opened.
Some will look for their name and won't find it there.

What a terrible time that will be!

Help me to remember that scene
so I will do everything I can do
to see that more names are added to Your book!
God, may those pages be full!

Sow for yourselves righteousness, reap the fruit of unfailing love, and break up your unplowed ground; for it is time to seek the Lord, until He comes and showers righteousness on you. – from Hosea 10:12

Dear Lord:

I'm not a great gardener
but I know that I reap what I sow –
that radish seeds won't produce lettuce
and that if I plant potatoes,
I won't get tomatoes.

I know that before planting,
the ground needs to be turned over.

Lord,
plow up my heart!

Rid it of prickly wild thistles
that choke the good seed of righteousness.

Be my Gardener, Lord!
You have a green thumb!

And afterward, I will pour out My Spirit on all people. Your sons and daughters will prophesy, your old men will dream dreams, your young men will see visions. Even on My servants, both men and women, I will pour out My Spirit in those days. And everyone who calls on the name of the Lord will be saved. – from Joel 2:28-32

Dear Lord:

Thank You that *all* who call on Your name will be saved!
I have called!

And You tell me that
my sons and daughters will prophesy
and I think that's wonderful!

You say that old men will have dreams
and I think that's amazing!

You say that young men will have visions
and I think that's glorious!

What about *old women*, Lord?
You don't specifically mention them.

But I am included
when You pour out Your Spirit!

That's marvelous!
I couldn't ask
for anything more
for *this* old woman!

"The days are coming," declares the Sovereign Lord, "when I will send a famine through the land – not a famine of food or a thirst for water, but a famine of hearing the words of the Lord. Men will stagger from sea to sea and wander from north to east, searching for the word of the Lord, but they will not find it." – from Amos 8:11-12

Dear Sovereign Lord:

What a famine that will be
when Your Word
will not be found!

Will those who then search
for Your message
find silence
because they have hardened their hearts
and spurned Your salvation?

Oh dear Lord,
I can't even imagine
such a famine!

Your silence
would be deathly!

The pride of your heart has deceived you, you who live in the clefts of the rocks and make your home on the heights, you say to yourself, "Who can bring me down to the ground?" Though you soar like the eagle and make your nest among the stars, from there I will bring you down," declares the Lord. – from Obadiah 3-4

Dear Lord:

One day,
proud as an eagle,
I built my nest on the tallest cliff.

In my arrogance
I thought I was a
big bird
living in a lofty place.
Who would dare to reach up
and disturb me.

Then one day,
Lord,
You reached down
and
feathers
flew!

Jonah went out and sat down at a place east of the city. There he made himself a shelter, sat in its shade and waited to see what would happen to the city. Then the Lord God provided a vine and made it grow up over Jonah to give shade for his head to ease his discomfort, and Jonah was very happy about the vine. But at dawn the next day God provided a worm, which chewed the vine so that it withered. When the sun arose, God provided a scorching east wind and the sun blazed on Jonah's head so that he grew faint. He wanted to die, and said, "It would be better for me to die than to live." – from Jonah 4:5-8

Dear Lord:

Jonah seemed excessively upset about a worm-eaten vine!

But there have been worms that have eaten my vines
and I didn't like it either!

I prayed that some early bird would get the worm!

I wailed, whined, fretted and fussed
half the day about
worms!

Lord,
may I be a lot *less* concerned
when I see a *worm* devouring the life of a plant!
It *isn't* the end of the world!

May I be a lot *more* concerned
when I see the *serpent* destroying the life of a person!
It *is* the end of the world!

But you, Bethlehem Ephrathah, though you are small among the clans of Judah, out of you will come for me One who will be ruler over Israel, whose origins are from of old, from ancient times. He will stand and shepherd His flock in the strength of the Lord, in the majesty of the name of the Lord His God. And they will live securely, for then His greatness will reach to the ends of the earth. And He will be their peace. – from Micah 5:2-5

Dear God:

From the little town of Bethlehem came
The Mighty One!
The Messiah!
The Lamb of God!

In a humble stable was born
The Fairest Ruler!
The Truest Peacemaker!
The Greatest King!
The Gentlest Shepherd!
The Savior!

Thank You, God,
for sending Your Beloved Son in the manner You did.

By that I know that one doesn't have to be born
in the largest city
or biggest home
or to the wealthiest family
to be Your child
and be blessed by You!

He has shown you, O man, what is good. And what does the Lord require of you? To act justly and to love mercy and to walk humbly with your God. – from Micah 6:8

Dear Lord God:

With all my heart I want to walk with You
and keep to Your pace.

Yet there are times
when I catch myself
lagging behind or out of step
with justice and mercy –
and I find myself walking proudly –
alone!

Lord God,
I don't enjoy walking alone.

Keep me on the right road,
going in the right direction,
and in step with You.

May I keep Your constant cadence of
justice,
humility,
and mercy.

Mercy! Those are big boots!

Who is a God like You, who pardons sin and forgives the transgression of the remnant of His inheritance? You do not stay angry forever but delight to show mercy. You will again have compassion on us; You will tread our sins underfoot and hurl all our iniquities into the depths of the sea. – from Micah 7:18-19

Dear God:

I like the way You forgive!
You pardon with mercy and love.

You tread my sins under Your feet
until they are like dust
and then You throw the dust
into the deepest sea!

And Lord,
I'm glad You aren't a deep-sea diver!

You forgive
without
ever –
in this world or the next –
slinging my soggy, salty sins
back in my face.

Thank You, Lord,
for deep-sea forgiveness!

The Lord is good, a refuge in times of trouble.   He cares for those who trust in Him.   – from Nahum 1:7

Dear Lord:

Thank You for being a God who cares
and is a shelter in the storm!

I can't conceive of
You
being any other kind of God!

But there are other *so-called* gods
who, it is said,
do evil
and bring trouble
to those who worship them.

Dear Lord,
thank you for being my kind of God!

I want no other!

How long, O Lord, must I call for help, but You do not listen? Or cry out to You, "Violence!" but You do not save? Why do You make me look at injustice? Why do You tolerate wrong? – from Habakkuk 1:2-3

Dear Lord:

Along with others, I have asked You,
"Why do some get away with murder?"
"Why does evil seem to win over good?"
"How long will You tolerate injustice?"

And then I remember
that Your purposes are eternal
while mine are temporary.

In *Your* time,
You will stand and shake the earth
and make the nations tremble.

There will come a day
when You will punish the wicked
and reward those who live by faith.

You said,
"I am going to do something in your day
that you would not believe,
even if you were told."

You, the *Believable* God,
will do the *unbelievable!*

The Lord your God is with you, He is mighty to save.   He will take great delight in you, He will quiet you with His love, He will rejoice over you with singing.   – from Zephaniah 3:17

Dear Lord God:

It sounds crazy to me
that *You,*
Almighty, Eternal, Holy God,
would save me, delight in me,
love and care for me,
and rejoice over me - with singing!

Who am *I* that You would do this?

Yet
because
of Your
˙divine
love and
mercy
which passes human understanding,
You have declared over and over and over
that *this* is
exactly
what
You
do –
and
You
proved
it on a
cross!

This is what the Lord Almighty says: "These people say, 'The time has not yet come for the Lord's house to be built.'" Then the word of the Lord came through the prophet Haggaï: "Is it a time for you yourselves to be living in your paneled houses, while this house remains a ruin?" Now this is what the Lord Almighty says: "Give careful thought to your ways. You have planted much, but have harvested little. You eat, but never have enough. You drink, but never have your fill. You put on clothes, but are not warm. You earn wages, only to put them in a purse with holes in it." – from Haggai 1:2-6

Dear Lord Almighty:

So that's why my hard-earned money
keeps disappearing!

I put it in a holey purse –
or is it an *unholy* one?

I told myself
that after *my* kingdom is complete,
then *Your* kingdom will get my attention.

But my excuse
is shot full of holes –
and so is my purse!

"On that day," declares the Lord Almighty, "I will take you, my servant Zerubbabel son of Shealtiel," declares the Lord, "and I will make you like my signet ring, for I have chosen you," declares the Lord Almighty. – from Haggai 2:23

Dear Lord Almighty:

I'd like to be Your signet ring,
chosen from among Your gems
to be worn by You!

I hope I'd be a ring of pure gold –
not a cheap imitation
that would turn Your finger green
and cause irritation.

Lord,
to be a ring on Your finger
would be glorious!

How wonderful it would be
to hear You say,
"I have her twisted around My little finger!"

*For this is what the Lord Almighty says: "After he has honored me
and has sent me against the nations that have plundered you – for
whoever touches you touches the apple of His eye – I will surely raise
My hand against them."* – from Zechariah 2:8,9

Dear Lord Almighty:

You declare that all Your children
are the apple of Your eye.

I'm so glad to be an apple!

Anyone who is the apple of Your eye
is precious and protected
and loved by You!

Therefore,
You warn me
to be very careful
what I do to the *other* apples –
even if I believe some of them are lemons!

Today, Lord,
I heard You ask me,
"How do you like them apples?"

This is what the Lord Almighty says: "Once again men and women of ripe old age will sit in the streets of Jerusalem, each with cane in hand because of his age. The city streets will be filled with boys and girls playing there." - from Zechariah 8:4-5

Dear Lord Almighty:

What a picture You painted –
children playing in the streets
being watched by old people,
each with a cane.

Lord,
as I shuffle out into the street
with my cane
to watch the children play,
keep me sweet –

and
if I ever *raise* cane,
may it be *sugar* cane!

I FIND THAT HARD TO BELIEVE _____

"When you bring blind animals for sacrifice, is that not wrong? When you sacrifice crippled or diseased animals, is that not wrong? Try offering them to your governor! Would he be pleased with you? Would he accept you?" says the Lord Almighty. – from Malachi 1:8

Dear Lord Almighty:

Sometimes I have given You
less than my best – such as:

a half-dollar in the offering
when I could have given more –

a half-hour of my time
when I could have given more –

a half-hearted effort
when I should have given more –

and I said to You,
*"Lord, would You believe
this is my sacrificial gift?"*

And I heard You reply,
"I find that hard to believe!"

Jesus said, *"You have heard that it was said to the people long ago, 'Do not murder, and anyone who murders will be subject to judgment.' But I tell you that anyone who is angry with his brother will be subject to judgment. You have heard that it was said, 'Do not commit adultery.' But I tell you that anyone who looks at a woman lustfully has already committed adultery with her in his heart. You have heard that it was said, 'Eye for eye, and tooth for tooth.' But I tell you, Do not resist an evil person. If someone strikes you on the right cheek, turn to him the other also. And if someone wants to sue you and take your tunic, let him have your cloak as well. If someone forces you to go one mile, go with him two miles."* - from Matthew 5:21-41

Dear Lord Jesus:

As I travel life's road, I've never yet thought of murder.
I've never even been awfully angry!
(But then, what level of anger are we talking about, Lord?)

And maybe I'm an *odd* bird
or an *old* bird with a poor memory,
but I can't remember even thinking of adultery!
(But then, what level of lust are we talking about, Lord?)

As I've traveled along,
for a fleeting moment I *have* thought of vengeance –
maybe not an eye for an eye, but
"an insult for an insult!"

Oh Lord, keep my heart pure at every level.

Be with me on my lonely journey
as I turn my left cheek, give up my cloak
and travel the second mile!

Lord, You've been down this road
and You know there's not much traffic there!

SUNKEN TREASURES

Jesus said, *"Do not store up for yourselves treasures on earth, where moth and rust destroy, and where thieves break in and steal. But store up for yourselves treasures in heaven, where moth and rust do not destroy and where thieves do not break in and steal. For where your treasure is, there your heart will be also."* – from Matthew 6:19-20

Dear Lord Jesus:

Over the years, things I once considered very important
have become sunken treasures!

The school picture is faded.
The Christmas gift is worn.
The diploma is crinkled.
The orchard is now a subdivision.
The dogwood tree is dead.
The corsage is dried up.
The woolen garment is moth-eaten.
The car is rusty.
The house needs remodeling.
The stock market has slumped and the bank has closed!
And maybe worse yet:
The skin is wrinkled.
The strength is gone.
The eyesight is dim.
The hearing is dull,
and the mind no longer remembers!

But because Your Spirit is alive and strong within me,
my soul's eye sees You better
and my soul's ear hears You better
with each passing year.

You, Lord, are my *unsinkable* Everlasting Treasure!

Jesus said, *"Therefore I tell you, do not worry about your life, what you will eat or drink; or about your body, what you will wear. Is not life more important than food, and the body more important than clothes? Look at the birds of the air; they do not sow or reap or store away in barns, and yet your heavenly Father feeds them. Are you not much more valuable than they?"* – from Matthew 6:25-26

Dear Lord God:

You said not to worry
about what I will put into my mouth.

You, the Creator,
provide for Your creation
and by the looks of *this* creature,
Your supply has been abundant!

You ask that I consider the birds.
They have no pantry packed with cans of worms,
no freezer full of fruit,
no satchel of suet,
no sacks of seeds,
no bags of bugs!

Yet they do not worry. They know You will feed them.

Then why should I ask,
"What will I eat?
When will I eat?
Where will I eat?
How much can I eat?
Will it be all-I-can-eat?"

God, You say these worries aren't even for the birds!

Jesus said, *"And why do you worry about clothes? See how the lilies of the field grow. They do not labor or spin. Yet I tell you that not even Solomon in all his splendor was dressed like one of these. If that is how God clothes the grass of the field, which is here today and tomorrow is thrown into the fire, will He not much more clothe you, O you of little faith?"* – from Matthew 6:28-30

Dear Lord Jesus:

One day You asked me,
"Why do you worry about clothes?"

I don't know!
I've never worried about being naked -
for my closet is crowded!

My worry has been about such things as,
"Is this outfit appropriate?"
"Is this still in style?"
"Will someone else be wearing the exact same thing?"

You said to remember the lilies of the field.
The lilies don't care if they are dressed alike,
and those bloomers are never out of style!
What a lily wears is always appropriate!

You said that God will clothe me
much *more* than He does the lilies of the field,
so there's no need
for a big walk-in closet
unless, of course, it's for prayer!

Jesus said, *"Which of you, if his son asks for bread, will give him a stone? Or if he asks for a fish, will give him a snake? If you, then, though you are evil, know how to give good gifts to your children, how much more will your Father in heaven give good gifts to those who ask Him!"* – from Matthew 7:9-11

Dear Father in Heaven:

I'm not afraid to ask for bread when I'm hungry,
for You've never served up a stone –
though I've eaten some pretty hard biscuits
served up by *other* folks!

I cannot even imagine
that You would dish up a snake
when I've prayed for a fish!
What a surprise that would be!

Your gifts are always good
and the only reason You may not give me what I ask for
is when I ask
for a rock that would weigh me down
or for a serpent that would bite!

But dear God,
when I pray for a fish,
may I remember You are *more* than a fisherman –
and when I pray for bread,
may I remember You are *more* than a baker!

You are my loving Father!

*Jesus replied, "Foxes have holes and birds of the air have nests, but
the Son of Man has no place to lay His head."* – from Matthew 8:20

Dear Creator Jesus:

You teach foxes how to dig their homes
and the sparrows how to build their nests.

Yet You had no place to lay Your head.

Even when You entered this world,
there was no room in the Inn.

Oh Lord,
if I would have been there,
You would have had a place!

Or would You?

I did not invite You into my heart
when You first knocked.
I did not allow You to enter my life
when You first called.

But then one day I said,
"Come in, Lord Jesus!"

I had Open House for You.

My heart had been empty long enough!

Knowing their thoughts, Jesus said, "Why do you entertain evil thoughts in your hearts?" – from Matthew 9:4

Dear Jesus:

May I *not* entertain evil thoughts
or welcome them
or be hospitable to them
or make them feel at home –
even for a moment!

May the plumbing of my heart be clean,
for pure water doesn't flow from dirty pipes.

And why should I be surprised
to find alligators lurking in my mind
if I'm living in the swamp?

Clean the pipes, Lord.
Drain the swamp!

May I live so close to You
that an evil thought
will not be allowed in,
no matter how it is disguised!

MORE THAN SPARROWS

Jesus said, *"Are not two sparrows sold for a penny? Yet not one of them will fall to the ground apart from the will of your Father. And even the very hairs of your head are all numbered. So don't be afraid; you are worth more than many sparrows."* – from Matthew 10:29-31

Dear Father God:

I'm glad that to *You*
I am worth *more* than many sparrows
sold in the marketplace!

One sparrow may be worth only half-a-penny to others,
and yet it cannot fall in its flight without Your notice.

Most likely You even tally its feathers,
for You number the hairs of my head.
You *add* new hairs and *subtract* fallen ones.
You *multiply*
those that have turned white with my worry!
But I doubt that You *divide* them,
for You don't split hairs!

Others may not give two cents for me
but You purchased me with the blood of Jesus!
What a price You paid for *this* old bird!

Why then should I worry about my feathers
or let others ruffle them?

Jesus told them another parable: "The kingdom of heaven is like a man who sowed good seed in his field. But while everyone was sleeping, his enemy came and sowed weeds among the wheat, and went away. When the wheat sprouted and formed heads, then the weeds also appeared. The servants asked him, 'Do you want us to go and pull them up?' 'No,' he answered, 'because while you are pulling the weeds, you may root up the wheat with them. Let both grow together until the harvest. At that time I will tell the harvesters: First collect the weeds and tie them in bundles to be burned, then gather the wheat and bring it into my barn.'" – from Matthew 13:24-30

Dear Lord Jesus:

Thank You for the lessons You have taught me regarding
weeds, goats and skunks!

You said if I walk into the field
and pull up wicked weeds,
in the process I'll pull up wonderful wheat!
My pulling isn't exact.

And if I walk up the hillside
and throw a rock at a graceless goat,
in the process I'll hit a lovely lamb!
My aim isn't perfect!

Lord, may I remember that *You* know best
how and when to separate
wheat from weeds
and sheep from goats
and what to do about skunks.

Whenever *I've* kicked a skunk
I've stunk
to highest heaven!

Jesus said, *"Woe to you, teachers of the law and Pharisees, you hypocrites! You give a tenth of your spices – mint, dill and cummin. But you have neglected the more important matters of the law – justice, mercy and faithfulness. You should have practiced the latter, without neglecting the former."* – from Matthew 23:23

Dear Jesus:

When the Scribes and Pharisees
presented their tithes
of spices,
You said there was something *more* than spices!

How often have I given a tenth,
carefully measured out:
my *mint* of minutes,
my *dill* of dollars,
my *cummin* of contributions.

Spices are easy to measure to the tenth.

Not so easily measured are
justice,
mercy
and faithfulness.

May I pour them out without measuring!

Now *that* would spice up my life!

Jesus said to the Scribes and Pharisees, *"You blind guides! You strain out a gnat but swallow a camel."* – from Matthew 23:24

Dear Jesus:

How often
have I choked
on a barely visible gnat
while
swallowing a double-humped camel?

How often
have I overlooked
the large unclean beast of my sin
while being bugged
about someone else's minor fault?

Lord,
forgive me
for being a nit-picker!

That
must be rather hard
for *You*
to swallow!

When Jesus was asked which of all the commandments was the most important, He answered: *"Hear, O Israel, the Lord our God, the Lord is one. Love the Lord your God with all your heart and with all your soul and with all your mind and with all your strength. The second is this: Love your neighbor as yourself. There is no commandment greater than these." "Well said, Teacher,"* the man replied. *"To love Him with all your heart, with all your understanding, and with all your strength, and to love your neighbor as yourself is more important than all burnt offerings and sacrifices."* – from Mark 12:29-33

Dear Lord Jesus:

You answered the question
about which is the most important commandment.
You said it is to love God
with all the heart and soul and mind and strength.

Then the man who asked the question
repeated Your answer, Jesus,
except
he left out loving God
with all his *soul*.

This must have been just a slip-of-the-tongue, Lord,
for it is said he answered wisely.

But I want my *soul* to be included, too!
I want to love You
with all I've got left of my mind and strength,
and with all my heart *and soul!*

I don't want to have a *slip-of-the-soul*!

Jesus sat down opposite the place where the offerings were put and watched the crowd putting their money into the temple treasury. Many rich people threw in large amounts. But a poor widow came and put in two very small copper coins, worth only a fraction of a penny. Calling His disciples to Him, Jesus said, "I tell you the truth, this poor widow has put more into the treasury than all the others. They all gave out of their wealth; but she, out of her poverty, put in everything - all she had to live on." - from Mark 12:41-44

Dear Lord Jesus:

I've often thought how wonderful it would be
to be rich,
and merrily, gleefully, joyfully
throw *big money* into an offering plate!

I wonder if I had been that poor widow
if I would have given my two small copper coins?
Or would I have thought,
"My gift is so small it won't count anyway" -
especially after watching the *big* givers?

Lord, did You call this to the attention of Your disciples
because they, too, were more impressed
by those who were giving *big money?*

You declared that the one who really gave *big* money
was the poor widow!

Lord, are You still watching
what's put in the offering plates,
and whether it is given out of
surplus or sacrifice?

Taking the five loaves and the two fish and looking up to heaven, Jesus gave thanks and broke them. Then He gave them to the disciples to set before the people. (About five thousand men were there.) They all ate and were satisfied, and the disciples picked up twelve basketfuls of broken pieces that were left over. – from Luke 9:16-17

Dear Lord Jesus:

When You divided
five loaves of bread and two fish,
there was *more* than enough
to feed about five thousand hungry men,
besides women and children.

Only *You*
could start with one small basket of food,
feed thousands,
and end up with twelve baskets of leftovers.

What did You do
with the leftovers, Lord?

Did Your disciples
make a lot of fish cakes?

Now that same day two of them were going to a village called Emmaus, about seven miles from Jerusalem. They were talking with each other about everything that had happened. As they talked and discussed these things with each other, Jesus Himself came up and walked along with them; but they were kept from recognizing Him. As they approached the village to which they were going, Jesus acted as if He were going farther. But they urged Him strongly, "Stay with us, for it is nearly evening; the day is almost over." So He went in to stay with them. When He was at the table with them, He took bread, gave thanks, broke it and began to give it to them. Then their eyes were opened and they recognized Him. – from Luke 24:13-31

Dear Lord Jesus:

You appear at places I wouldn't expect:
on the road to Emmaus,
on the road through Samaria,
on the road to Simon the sinner's house,
on the road to the home of Zaccheus, the tax collector,
and on the road to Damacus.

Lord,
on my earthly journey,
I've stopped and looked for You in
churches, chapels and cathedrals –
but because I wasn't expecting You on the highway
I passed You and didn't know it!

Lord God,
may I slow down
and keep my eyes wide open on the road!

FISHY EXCUSE

When Jesus looked up and saw a great crowd coming toward Him, He said to Philip, "Where shall we buy bread for these people to eat?" He asked this only to test him, for He already had in mind what He was going to do. Philip answered Him, "Eight month's wages would not buy enough bread for each one to have a bite!" Another of His disciples, Andrew, Simon Peter's brother, spoke up, "Here is a boy with five small barley loaves and two small fish, but how far will they go among so many?" Jesus said, "Have the people sit down." There was plenty of grass in that place, and the men sat down, about five thousand of them. Jesus then took the loaves, gave thanks, and distributed to those who were seated as much as they wanted. He did the same with the fish. – John 6:5-11

Dear Jesus:

When You fed thousands of people
with a boy's lunch of bread and fish,
I believe that was the *third* miracle of the day!

The *first* miracle
was that the boy hadn't already eaten his lunch!
Some little boys couldn't have waited.

The *second* miracle
was that the lad was willing to share his fish and bread.
Some young lads would worry
that they wouldn't have enough for themselves!

Lord Jesus,
some time ago You asked a not-so-young lady
to share what she had.
She gave the alibi
that she wouldn't have enough left for herself.

Lord, did my excuse smell fishy?

Yet at the same time many even among the leaders believed in Him. But because of the Pharisees they would not confess their faith for fear they would be put out of the synagogue; for they loved praise from men more than praise from God.   – from John 12:42-43

Lord Jesus:

When You lived among us here on earth,
some didn't make public confession of You
because they loved praise from men
more than
praise from God.

When it comes to praise from men,
often there's a loud *"BRAVO!"*

When it comes to praise from You,
often there's a quiet *"Well done."*

But Lord,
praise from men
is as fickle as a weathervane!

Praise from You is sure
no matter which way the wind is blowing!

Jesus said, "I will not leave you as orphans; I will come to you. Before long, the world will not see Me anymore, but you will see Me. Because I live, you also will live." — from John 14:18-19

Dear Jesus:

Thank You
for not leaving me as an orphan
when You left this earth.

You come to me
and I see You
with the eyes of my soul.

You speak to me
and tell me I am Your child,
and You promise to be with me always.

Why,
then,
should my countenance
be sad
as though
I'm
some
God-forsaken
orphan?

Jesus said, *"I am the true vine and My Father is the gardener. He cuts off every branch in Me that bears no fruit, while every branch that does bear fruit He trims clean so that it will be even more fruitful.*
- from John 15:1-2

Dear Gardener God:

Pardon me for saying so,
but what goes on in Your vineyard sounds painful!

If there's *no* fruit on my branch,
I will be cut off!
I must have *more* than leaves
or I'll feel the Gardener's knife!

If there *is* fruit,
I get a trimming!
I must have *more* than a little fruit
or I'll feel the pruning shears!

Dear Gardener God,
help me stay firmly connected to the True Vine,
that I may bear bushels of the best fruit!

And when I begin to think
my fruit is extra fancy –
You will trim me back to size!

When they had finished eating, Jesus said to Simon Peter, "Simon son of John, do you truly love Me more than these?"   "Yes, Lord," he said, "You know that I love You."   Jesus said, "Feed My lambs." Again Jesus said, "Simon son of John, do you truly love Me?"   He answered, "Yes, Lord, You know that I love You."   Jesus said, "Take care of My sheep."   The third time He said to him, "Simon son of John, do you love Me?"   Peter was hurt because Jesus asked him the third time, "Do you love Me?" He said, "Lord, You know all things; You know that I love You." Jesus said, "Feed My sheep."   Then He said to him, "Follow Me!"   – from John 21:15-19

Dear Lord Jesus:

When You asked Peter to look after Your sheep,
I wonder if he said to himself,
*"I'd rather not mess with sheep!
I'm a fisherman – not a shepherd!"*

And You may also say to me,
"Feed my lambs and sheep and take care of them."

I'm not a shepherd *or* a fisherman
and I may say to myself,
*"Sheep and lambs can be smelly and dumb.
Maybe they won't eat what I feed them!
Maybe one will wander away and get lost!
Do I have to risk my life for a dumb, lost sheep?"*

But before I can protest, You, the Good Shepherd,
show me a picture of a lost, dirty, dumb sheep
that looks just like me –
being gently carried in the arms of a Shepherd
that looks exactly like You,
coming from a hill called Calvary.

So Peter was kept in prison, but the church was earnestly praying to God for him. The night before Herod was to bring him to trial, Peter was sleeping between two soldiers, bound with two chains, and sentries stood guard at the entrance. Suddenly an angel of the Lord appeared and a light shone in the cell. He struck Peter on the side and woke him up. "Quick, get up!" he said, and the chains fell off Peter's wrists. – from Acts 12:5-7

Dear Lord God:

I have always pictured angels
as gentle, meek and mild.
That's the way some artists draw them,
floating serenely in the sky,
or standing calmly in the background,
or gently kissing the brow of a child.

But the angel who was sent
to free Peter from prison
slapped him.
Maybe Peter was a sound sleeper.

And maybe angels would have a hard time
getting *my* attention.

Lord,
when I need to be freed from some prison,
and I'm sleeping or not listening,
have Your angel slap me along side of the head!

I want to be free!

On the first day of the week, we came together to break bread. Paul spoke to the people and, because he intended to leave the next day, kept on talking until midnight. Seated in a window was a young man named Eutychus, who was sinking into a deep sleep as Paul talked on and on. When he was sound asleep, he fell to the ground from the third story and was picked up dead. Paul went down, threw himself on the young man and put his arms around him. "Don't be alarmed," he said. "He's alive!" Then he went upstairs again and broke bread and ate. After talking until daylight, he left. – from Acts 20:7 & 9-11

Dear Lord:

I doubt that young Eutychus
was the only one who fell asleep
when the Apostle Paul preached until midnight –

but he was probably the only one
perched on a windowsill!

When Eutychus fell from his window seat,
Paul left the pulpit
and went three stories below
to revive the dead young man.
I wonder if Eutychus
ever again sat on a windowsill?

Lord, keep me wide awake
as I listen to Your Word
and help me find a safer seat,
especially if the preacher goes until midnight!

That's a lot of stories!

You see, at just the right time, when we were still powerless, Christ died for the ungodly. Very rarely will anyone die for a righteous man, though for a good man someone might possibly dare to die. But God demonstrates His own love for us in this: While we were still sinners, Christ died for us. – from Romans 5:6-8

Dear Savior God:

One of my favorite old songs says:

"Amazing love,
how can it be,
that Thou, my God,
shouldst die for me. "

I'll never understand it,
never fully grasp
why a godly God
would die
for
ungodly me!

But You said it was a
demonstration
of Your love!

I've never before seen such a display!

Since we have now been justified by His blood, how much more shall we be saved from God's wrath through Him! For if, when we were God's enemies, we were reconciled to Him through the death of His Son, how much more, having been reconciled, shall we be saved through His life! – from Romans 5:9-10

Dear Lord Jesus:

Thank you
for the case of *much mores*
which You delivered!

Much more
shall I be saved from sin
through Your death.

Much more
shall I be saved from wrath
through Your life.

Much more
shall God's grace
overflow to many, including me!

Much more
than I deserve!

The creation waits in eager expectation for the sons of God to be revealed. For the creation was subjected to frustration, not by its own choice, but by the will of the one who subjected it, in hope that the creation itself will be liberated from its bondage to decay and brought into the glorious freedom of the children of God. We know that the whole creation has been groaning as in the pains of childbirth right up to the present time. – from Romans 8:19-22

Dear God:

All the woods appeared dead on a cool April morn,
as I walked through wet leaves on a path all forlorn.
Not a flower had risen from winter's cold grave,
though the sun seemed to coax all the earth to be brave.

I returned to the woods on a warm day in May,
and sensed You had been there as I walked down the way.
For like flags in the wind the new leaves had unfurled,
and the flowers from deep in the earth had been hurled.

Purple violets and trilliums did carpet the floor
and above me the dogwood had blossomed once more.
What appeared to be dead on a cool April morn,
was alive now in May as a woods was reborn.

Dear God,
I pray others may sense
that You have walked down the path of my soul!

For no one can lay any foundation other than the one already laid, which is Jesus Christ. If any man builds on this foundation using gold, silver, costly stones, wood, hay or straw, his work will be shown for what it is, because the Day will bring it to light. It will be revealed with fire, and the fire will test the quality of each man's work. – from I Corinthians 3:11-13

Dear Jesus:

When my work is finished here
and someday goes through the fire,
will anything I've done survive?

It's possible, I suppose, to use
wood, hay and straw,
and make it *look* as if it were
gold, silver and precious stones.

But the fire won't be fooled!

Lord Jesus,
may I remember
that the building material I choose today
will tomorrow be in the fire!

I pray that what I do for You
will be more than big bangs and glittering lights
which last only a brief moment.
After the fireworks,
may what remains
be more than a few clinkers
on Your beautiful foundation!

The body is a unit, though it is made up of many parts; and though all its parts are many, they form one body. So it is with Christ.. If the whole body were an eye, where would the sense of hearing be? If the whole body were an ear, where would the sense of smelling be? But in fact God has arranged the parts in the body, every one of them, just as He wanted them to be. If they were all one part, where would the body be? – from I Corinthians 12:12-19

Dear Lord Christ:

Sometimes it appears that Your Body
has become disconnected from You, the Head.
Like a headless horseman
the Church gallops on its way,
not seeing, hearing or obeying You.

Even the Body's members
become disjointed
one from the other.
We think we don't need some parts.

Therefore, a gigantic eye
or enormous elbow
or colossal foot
tries to convince a lost world
that *this* is the Church –
and unbelievers stare at us in disbelief!

Oh Lord,
when the world looks at Your Body,
may it *not* see
just one big heel!

If I speak in the tongues of men and of angels, but have not love, I am only a resounding gong or a clanging cymbal. If I have the gift of prophecy and can fathom all mysteries and all knowledge, and if I have a faith that can move mountains, but have not love, I am nothing. If I give all I possess to the poor and surrender my body to the flames, but have not love, I gain nothing. – from I Corinthians 13:1-3

Dear Lord God:

You said there is something greater
than speaking in other tongues,
prophesying,
revealing mysteries,
having knowledge,
moving mountains,
sacrificing,
and dying a martyr's death!

You said *love* is *greater* than these!

On life's stage,
have I been
banging gongs and clanging cymbals
while *love* has been left waiting in the wings?

Lord,
help me to move *love* to center stage
and let *You* do the directing!

Otherwise,
the curtain is coming down
and the play is over!

The Apostle Paul wrote: *Are they servants of Christ? I am more. I have worked much harder, been in prison more frequently, been flogged more severely, and been exposed to death again and again. Five times I received from the Jews the forty lashes minus one. Three times I was beaten with rods, once I was stoned, three times I was shipwrecked, I spent a night and a day in the open sea, I have been constantly on the move. I have been in danger from rivers, in danger from bandits, in danger from my own countrymen, in danger from Gentiles; in danger in the city, in danger in the country, in danger at sea; and in danger from false brothers. I have labored and toiled and have often gone without sleep; I have known hunger and thirst, and have often gone without food; I have been cold and naked. Besides everything else, I face daily the pressure of my concern for all the churches.* – from II Corinthians 11:23-28

Dear Lord Jesus:

I am weakened by weakness, insulted by insults,
discouraged by difficulties and unhappy with hardships.
I wonder if Your grace is truly sufficient?
Has it been road tested
and proven on the test track of life?

And I hear You whisper to me,
*"Yes – it's been road tested and proven on the test track
by the Apostles and many other believers –
and by Me!"*

Ah yes, Lord Jesus! Your grace has been road tested
and proven sufficient
in flogging, burning, stoning, beating, beheading,
banishment, persecution, shipwreck –
and crucifixion!

When I think of *You*, Lord Jesus, and the Apostle Paul,
my problems are nothing more than a
slight inconvenience!

The Apostle Paul wrote, *"My dear children, for whom I am again in the pains of childbirth until Christ is formed in you, how I wish I could be with you now and change my tone, because I am perplexed about you!"* – from Galatians 4:19

Dear God:

With the Apostle Paul
my dear mother could have said about me,
*"I am in the pains of childbirth
until Christ is formed in you."*

And with Saint Paul
I echo those same words
regarding my children and grandchildren.

It is like the pain of childbirth
as a parent writhes
over the spiritual birth of a child.

And it is like the pleasure of childbirth
as a parent witnesses
the spiritual birth of a child.

Singing replaces sighing
and laughter replaces lamentation
as a child or grandchild
is born into God's family and grows in His grace.

God's grace is worth the groans!

Consequently, you are no longer foreigners and aliens but fellow citizens with God's people and members of God's household, built on the foundation of the apostles and prophets, with Christ Jesus Himself as the chief cornerstone. In Him the whole building is joined together and rises to become a holy temple in the Lord. And in Him you too are being built together to become a dwelling in which God lives by His Spirit. – from Ephesians 2:19-22

Dear Jesus:

You have a building under construction,
and I'm glad I can be
one clay brick in Your holy temple.

You are not only the Chief Cornerstone,
but also the mortar
that holds everything together.

I wonder how the material supply is coming along?
I believe there are many more bricks
that need to be gathered,
salvaged from the wreckage.
I am thankful You take the broken ones,
reclaim them and fit them into Your building.

I know that in *You*, the Contractor and Supplier,
the whole building will be complete.

When *others* try to take over *Your* work,
they will always be
a few bricks short of a load!

Now to Him who is able to do immeasurably more than all we ask or imagine, according to His power that is at work within us, to Him be glory in the church and in Christ Jesus throughout all generations, for ever and ever! Amen. – from Ephesians 3:20-21

Dear Lord God Almighty:

Thank You for being able to do
immeasurably more
than I can ask
or imagine!

My imagination runs wild
and my requests are many,
though I've never asked
for the moon!

I am thankful
Your power never wanes!
Your strength never ebbs!
Your love never goes out with the tide!

Thank You for being my God
who is
*immeasurably
more than!*

But whatever was to my profit I now consider loss for the sake of Christ. What is more, I consider everything a loss compared to the surpassing greatness of knowing Christ Jesus my Lord, for whose sake I have lost all things. I consider them rubbish, that I may gain Christ and be found in Him, not having a righteousness of my own that comes from the law, but that which is through faith in Christ – the righteousness that comes from God and is by faith. I want to know Christ and the power of His resurrection and the fellowship of sharing in His sufferings, becoming like Him in his death, and so, somehow, to attain to the resurrection from the dead. – from Philippians 3:7-11

Dear Lord God:

I want my life's aim to be this:
to know You,
to gain You,
and to be found in You.

In comparison to You,
everything else is garbage
in the trash can!

Lord,
I pray that You will *not* find me
digging around in the dumpster,
sifting through the trash.

There are a few things in there that look good
until
I compare them to You!

Then I know they belong in the dumpster!

For I have learned to be content whatever the circumstances. I know what it is to be in need, and I know what it is to have plenty. I have learned the secret of being content in any and every situation, whether well fed or hungry, whether living in plenty or in want. I can do everything through Him who gives me strength. - from Philippians 4:11-13

Dear Lord God:

It's *not* difficult to be content
with good circumstances!

I've had times like that!
The lessons are easy
and I sail through them,
like a boat on sunny seas!

But to be content
in bad circumstances is a different story.

I've had times like that!
The lessons are hard
and I struggle through them,
like rowing a boat on stormy seas!

Lord, when I start to
rest on my *oars,*
may I remember the secret
is resting in *You!*

When you were dead in your sins and in the uncircumcision of your sinful nature, God made you alive with Christ. He forgave us all our sins, having canceled the written code with its regulations, that was against us and that stood opposed to us; He took it away, nailing it to the cross. And having disarmed the powers and authorities, He made a public spectacle of them, triumphing over them by the cross. –
from Colossians 2:13-15

Dear Lord Jesus:

Thank You for Your forgiveness
of all my sins
and for giving me eternal life.

Thank You for writing
CANCELED
with
Your blood
on the indictment against me!

Satan had me locked in his prison
until
You released me
with a key
in the shape of a cross!

Be wise in the way you act toward outsiders; make the most of every opportunity. Let your conversation be always full of grace, seasoned with salt, so that you may know how to answer everyone. – from Colossians 4:5-6

Dear Lord God:

You said to season my talk with salt
and that probably means just a little.

Often my conversation
is *full* of salt
and seasoned with just a *little* grace!

Lord,
help me to get it right!

A *lot* of grace!
A *little* salt.

May the way I live make people
thirsty for You,
the Living Water.

God forbid that my life
would be so salty
that I'd cause people to throw up!

Finally, brothers, we instructed you how to live in order to please God, as in fact you are living. Now we ask you and urge you in the Lord Jesus to do this more and more. Now about brotherly love we do not need to write to you, for you yourselves have been taught by God to love each other. And in fact, you do love all the brothers throughout Macedonia. Yet we urge you, brothers, to do so more and more. – from I Thessalonians 4:1-10

Dear Lord:

I want to love You today
more
than I did yesterday or last week or last year!

I want to please You today
more
than I did yesterday or last week or last year!

And help me, Lord,
to love others today
a lot more
than I did yesterday!

Yesterday I was a little irked with a friend!
I loved him
a lot less
than I did last week or last year!

Help me, Lord, more and more
with the *more and more* kind of love!

For the Lord Himself will come down from heaven, with a loud command, with the voice of the archangel and with the trumpet call of God, and the dead in Christ will rise first. After that, we who are still alive and are left will be caught up with them in the clouds to meet the Lord in the air. And so we will be with the Lord forever. Therefore encourage each other with these words. – from I Thessalonians 4:16-18

Dear Lord Jesus:

Someday there's going to be an event
that will beat all other events
and *You* are my ticket!

If I enter the gate with You,
I'll not need anything else!
You paid my full fare in advance!

I'm glad my reservation
is not like other reservations I've made,
only later to find that the airline had overbooked
and I was left waiting at the gate.

This reservation
is guaranteed and insured
by Your precious blood!

You said You would even take care of
my time of departure!

All I need to do is to be ready!

We hear that some among you are idle. They are not busy; they are busybodies. Such people we command and urge in the Lord Jesus Christ to settle down and earn the bread they eat. And as for you, brothers, never tire of doing what is right. – from II
Thessalonians 3:11-13

Dear Lord:

From the time of Saint Paul, at least,
there have been busybodies!

Sometimes they are called
meddlers,
troublemakers,
snoops,
people who poke their noses in other peoples' business.

No one seems to appreciate them!

Is *that* an understatement?

Lord,
help me keep this body busy
doing what is right.

Keep my nose
from picking up the wrong scent!

St. Paul wrote: *Here is a trustworthy saying that deserves full acceptance: Christ Jesus came into the world to save sinners – of whom I am the worst. But for that very reason I was shown mercy so that in me, the worst of sinners, Christ Jesus might display His unlimited patience as an example for those who would believe on Him and receive eternal life.* – from I Timothy 1:15-16

Dear Christ Jesus:

Saint Paul thought he was the *worst* sinner,
although others of us could possibly vie for that title.
Before Paul's conversion
he was the leading persecutor of Christians
and he was there for the stoning of Stephen.

But, Lord,
with Your foreknowledge
You knew that *Worst Sinner Saul*
would become *Greatest Saint Paul* –
and You saved him.

Also with Your foreknowledge
You knew that *Worst Sinner Vi*
would *never* become *Greatest Saint Vi* –
and yet You saved me!

What mercy!

St. Paul wrote to Timothy: *I have been reminded of your sincere faith, which first lived in your grandmother Lois and in your mother Eunice and, I am persuaded, now lives in you also.* – from II Timothy 1:5

Dear Lord God:

What a tribute to Timothy's grandmother and mother,
that they had a sincere faith
which was alive now in Timothy.

I can think of nothing better to pass along
to children and grandchildren
than a sincere faith in You,
the living Christ.

Lord,
give me power to walk with a convincing faith,
free of sham,
full of love,
so my children and grandchildren
will want to follow.

Houses, land, silver, gold, stocks, bonds,
or any other bequest
won't be worth a wooden nickel to them –
if they don't have *You!*

Teach the older men to be temperate, worthy of respect, self-controlled, and sound in faith, in love and in endurance. Likewise, teach the older women to be reverent in the way they live, not to be slanderers or addicted to much wine, but to teach what is good. – from Titus 2:2-3

Dear Lord God:

Does it seem odd
that You need to teach
older men
and older women
how to behave?

But then again, that's not odd!

With each passing year,
I become more and more forgetful.

Teach me again
to behave!

I want to be respectable,
saintly and sober,
without being an old stick-in-the-mud.

Lord,
I want to behave!

I always thank my God as I remember you in my prayers, because I hear about your faith in the Lord Jesus and your love for all the saints. I pray that you may be active in sharing your faith, so that you will have a full understanding of every good thing we have in Christ.
– from Philemon 4-6

Dear Lord Christ:

Nothing makes me more grateful
and more filled with joy
than to hear reports
that those I love
have faith.

And Lord,
nothing makes me more fearful
and more filled with concern
than to hear reports
that those I love
lack faith.

Often
faith in You
has appeared in those where I least suspected it –
and
been absent in those where I most expected it.

I plead, Lord Jesus,
that those who are now
absent in their faith
will be present.

In the Old Testament, *The blood of goats and bulls and the ashes of a heifer sprinkled on those who are ceremonially unclean sanctify them so that they are outwardly clean. How much more, then, will the blood of Christ, who through the eternal Spirit offered Himself unblemished to God, cleanse our consciences from acts that lead to death, so that we may serve the living God!* – from Hebrews 9:13-14

Dear God:

Thank You
that today I need not enter a temple
and offer a sacrifice of an animal
and have a priest sprinkle its blood on me
so that I may be *outwardly* clean!

Today I can enter Your presence
and accept Your sacrifice
and have You wash me with the blood of Your Son Jesus
so that I may be *inwardly* clean.

That's *much more* clean!

And dear God,
thank You that the blood never loses its power.
No matter how many of us sinners
You wash in the blood of Jesus,
it never loses its strength or its purity to cleanse.

That's absolute, perfect cleansing!

Remember those earlier days after you had received the light, when you stood your ground in a great contest in the face of suffering. Sometimes you were publicly exposed to insult and persecution; at other times you stood side by side with those who were so treated. You sympathized with those in prison and joyfully accepted the confiscation of your property, because you knew that you yourselves had better and lasting possessions. So do not throw away your confidence; it will be richly rewarded. You need to persevere so that when you have done the will of God, you will receive what He has promised. – from Hebrews 10:32-36

Dear Lord God:

I know that any sacrifice I make for You
will someday be rewarded.

Why, then, is *sacrifice* not something I do easily?

Or maybe I do –
when it's for some earthly reward such as
a lake cottage, newer car,
bigger house, nicer clothes,
longer vacation, better retirement.

These call for some type of sacrifice
in order to have them.
It often means working overtime, getting a second job,
doing without something else.

Sometimes the earthly reward
isn't all I imagined it would be.
Looking back, it *wasn't* worth the sacrifice!

But, Lord, when I sacrifice for You,
the reward will be *more* than I can imagine!
Looking ahead, it *will* be worth the sacrifice!

Through Jesus, therefore, let us continually offer to God a sacrifice of praise - the fruit of lips that confess His name. And do not forget to do good and to share with others, for with such sacrifices God is pleased. - from Hebrews 13:15-16

Dear Lord:

You have told me plainly
what kinds of sacrifices please You.

One of them would be that I give You
a Thank Offering continually,
not just once in awhile.
May I keep the thanksgiving fires burning
like an eternal flame!

And Lord,
You want more than lip service!

May the coals from Your altar
not only warm
my lips with praise,
but burn in my heart and hands
to serve others
and share with others -
for *Your* glory!

Consider it pure joy, my brothers, whenever you face trials of many kinds, because you know that the testing of your faith develops perseverance. Perseverance must finish its work so that you may be mature and complete, not lacking anything. – from James 1:2-4

Dear Lord Jesus:

You said I should consider it pure joy
when trials come.

I know they come,
ready or not!

But consider it *joy?*
Oh, boy!
That's something to consider!

Lord Jesus,
the only way I can consider it joy
is by looking back
at what You bore
for me –
and
by looking ahead
at what You are birthing
in me.

Lord,
may I remember that with *You*
I always get a fair trial!

All kinds of animals, birds, reptiles, and creatures of the sea are being tamed and have been tamed by man, but no man can tame the tongue. It is a restless evil, full of deadly poison. With the tongue we praise our Lord and Father, and with it we curse men, who have been made in God's likeness. My brothers, this should not be. – from James 3:7-10

Dear Lord:

You said all sorts of living things
have been tamed by man.

There are lions trained by lion tamers,
horses broken by riders,
dogs schooled by owners,
birds taught by teachers.

But there's something, Lord, that only *You* can tame!
It's a strange thing called the *tongue!*

I've tried to subdue this beast –
but it doesn't take easily to confinement
even when I attempt to keep the cage shut!

This wild and slippery creature often gets loose!
It slips the bridle and bites someone!

Lord,
catch it and tame it!
Tighten up the leash!

Only set it free
to sing Your praises and bless men!

Submit yourselves, then, to God. Resist the devil, and he will flee from you. Come near to God and He will come near to you. Humble yourselves before the Lord, and He will lift you up. – from James 4:7-10

Dear God:

Help me with my
submitting and resisting!

Sometimes I mess it up!

I submit to the devil
and resist You!

I fail to come near to You
and wonder why You seem so far away!

I am filled with pride
and wonder why You don't lift me up!

Lord,
I want to get it right!

I know You will come near to me
when I make a move toward You.

Lord, can we meet for dessert soon?
I'm now ready
for a large helping of humble pie!

Praise be to the God and Father of our Lord Jesus Christ! In His great mercy He has given us new birth into a living hope through the resurrection of Jesus Christ from the dead, and into an inheritance that can never perish, spoil or fade – kept in heaven for you, who through faith are shielded by God's power until the coming of the salvation that is ready to be revealed in the last time. – from I Peter 1:3-5

Dear Father God:

I'd like to shout, *"Yay, God!"*

Thank You for the resurrection of Your Son Jesus
through whom I have a living hope!
For if Christ had not come out of His tomb,
I know I would not be coming out of mine either!

There were people who thought they could,
with a big stone,
keep Jesus in the grave.

God, I'm glad that didn't work!

And because it didn't work,
I've not yet bought a grave.
I'm wanting only to *rent* one, when and if I need it!

For, by Your grace, if I use it at all,
it will be only for a short time - until the resurrection!

*"Yay, God! Oui, God! Ja, God! Sì, God!
Sí, God! Yo, God!
Yes, God!* in any language!

*In this you greatly rejoice, though now for a little while you may have
had to suffer grief in all kinds of trials. These have come so that your
faith - of greater worth than gold, which perishes even though refined
by fire - may be proved genuine and may result in praise, glory and
honor when Jesus Christ is revealed.* - from I Peter 1:6-7

Dear Lord God:

Thank You for a faith
that is worth *more* than gold!

I wonder, though,
if my faith
would be measured like gold,
would it be
12 carat,
14 carat,
or pure gold?

Is my faith real?
Is it authentic, actual, absolute?
Or is it like fool's gold -
flashy, fake, false?

If it's real gold,
fire will burn away impurities and produce beauty.

Oh, Lord,
is there any other way?
I hope so -
but if it takes the furnace,
at the height of the heat,
may I bring You praise, glory and honor.

PATIENCE! PATIENCE!

With the Lord a day is like a thousand years, and a thousand years are like a day. The Lord is not slow in keeping His promise, as some understand slowness. He is patient with you, not wanting anyone to perish, but everyone to come to repentance.   – from II Peter 3:8-9

Dear Lord:

Thank You for Your patience
with me!

If You were *not* patient –
not wanting me to perish –
I would have.

Why, then, am I impatient with others?

Why do I give up on them,
saying to myself,
"Well, I did all I could do!"

It's difficult for me to conceive of eternity
but I know it's a
long, long, long, long, long, long time!

Too long to be lost,
even for a moment!

Lord,
help me to be as patient with others
as You were with me!
I don't want anyone to perish either!

Dear friends, let us love one another, for love comes from God. Everyone who loves has been born of God and knows God. Whoever does not love does not know God, because God is love. This is how God showed His love among us: He sent His one and only Son into the world that we might live through Him. This is love: not that we loved God, but that He loved us and sent His Son as an atoning sacrifice for our sins. Dear friends, since God so loved us, we also ought to love one another. No one has ever seen God; but if we love each other, God lives in us and His love is made complete in us. - from I John 4:7-12

Dear Lord God:

You said that if I do *not* love,
I don't know You!

But what is *love?*

Sometimes love is described as
affection,
attachment,
desire,
passion,
devotion,
fondness,
adoration,
sacrifice.

But is there another word that better defines
true, pure, wonderful *love?*

Ah yes! *God!*

And this is love: that we walk in obedience to His commands. As you have heard from the beginning, His command is that you walk in love.
– from II John 6

Dear Lord Jesus:

Your commandment to me
is that I walk in love.

Sounds easy!

But as I put one foot in front of the other,
and begin to walk the path of love,
I often stumble.

Some days I fail to love You, Lord,
with *everything* I've got!

Some days I fail to love my neighbor
with *anything* I've got!

I whisper to myself,
"Maybe God didn't see that!
Maybe God didn't hear that!"

But then I hear You calling,
"Hey, Vi!"

Dear friend, do not imitate what is evil but what is good. Anyone who does what is good is from God. Anyone who does what is evil has not seen God. - from III John 11

Dear God,

Your words are clear and simple:
If I *have* seen You, I will do good.
If I do evil, I *haven't* seen You.

I know folks who wouldn't *bat an eye* at doing wrong,
but by Your grace I want to be good!
That requires that I see You!

Lord God,
correct the vision of my soul to at least 20/20.
Though age may take its toll on human eyesight,
may my soul not go blind
or lose its ability to focus on You.

Improve the astigmatism so I may have clarity of vision.
Remove the *badder-acts* from my eyes!

As I read the eye chart of Your Word,
I want to see more than just letters of the alphabet.
I want to see

G O D

Dear friends, although I was very eager to write to you about the salvation we share, I felt I had to write and urge you to contend for the faith that was once for all entrusted to the saints. – from Jude 3

Dear Lord God:

I don't know why You would,
once for all,
entrust the faith
to *anyone* here on earth,
even to the saintly!

But You did.

I wonder how You feel about that now?

I'm not a saint
(I didn't need to tell You that!)
but as a believer,
am I contending for the faith?

Or am I merely contentious?
Lord, I hope not!

I want to be trusted with the truth
and fight for the faith,
holding tight with all my might
to Your unchanging Word!

Enoch, the seventh from Adam, prophesied about these men: "See, the Lord is coming with thousands upon thousands of His holy ones to judge everyone, and to convict all the ungodly of all the ungodly acts they have done in the ungodly way, and of all the harsh words ungodly sinners have spoken against Him." These men are grumblers and faultfinders; they follow their own evil desires; they boast about themselves and flatter others for their own advantage. – from Jude 14-16

Dear Lord God:

Among the ungodly are listed
grumblers,
faultfinders,
boasters,
flatterers!

Forgive me, Lord God.

I've grumbled
and called it righteous indignation.

I've found fault
and called it being helpful.

I've boasted
and called it praising You.

I've flattered
and called it encouragement.

You call it ungodly!

But, dear friends, remember what the apostles of our Lord Jesus Christ foretold. They said to you, "In the last times there will be scoffers who will follow their own ungodly desires." These are men who divide you, who follow mere natural instincts and do not have the Spirit. But you, dear friends, build yourselves up in your most holy faith, and pray in the Holy Spirit. Keep yourselves in God's love as you wait for the mercy of our Lord Jesus Christ to bring you to eternal life. Be merciful to those who doubt; snatch others from the fire and save them. – from Jude 17-23

Dear Lord God of Heaven:

There are *some* folks You warn me about:
the scoffers and dividers,
who think only of themselves.

In spite of *these* folks I am to keep the faith,
keep in Your love, and pray.

Their scoffing *won't* upset
heaven's apple cart!

There are some *other* folks You warn me about:
the weak and lost
who need mercy and salvation.

In behalf of *these* folks I am to be merciful,
snatch them from the fire,
and save them.

Their salvation *will* upset
hell's apple cart!

To Him who loves us and has freed us from our sins by His blood, and has made us to be a kingdom and priests to serve His God and Father – to Him be glory and power for ever and ever! Amen. Look, He is coming with the clouds, and every eye will see Him, even those who pierced Him; and all the peoples of the earth will mourn because of Him. So shall it be! Amen! "I am the Alpha and the Omega," says the Lord God, "who is, and who was, and who is to come, the Almighty." – from Revelation 1:5-8

Dear Lord Jesus:

You have plans to come to earth again!

This time
You won't be a baby in a manger
where only a few people see You.

This time
every eye shall see You.

And in the Book of Revelation,
I read of a double-edged sword
and seven seals and seven trumpets,
of wars, famines, plagues, martyrdom,
of the moon turning to blood,
about a dragon and a beast
and other things that
scare me to death!

And I hear You say,
*"Let these things
scare you
to your knees!"*

*And I saw an angel coming down out of heaven, having the key to the
Abyss and holding in his hand a great chain. He seized the dragon,
that ancient serpent, who is the devil, or Satan, and bound him for a
thousand years. He threw him into the Abyss, and locked and sealed
it over him, to keep him from deceiving the nations any more until the
thousand years were ended. After that, he must be set free for a short
time. – from Revelation 20:1-3*

Lord God of Heaven:

There are so many things I don't understand
about the end of time, and this is one of them.

The angel will seize Satan,
bind him,
throw him into the bottomless pit,
lock him in
and seal him up –
but *only* for 1,000 years!

Then the devil is released!

Lord God,
while Satan is bound and gagged,
wouldn't it be a good idea
to throw him into the lake of fire right then and there,
and never let him loose again, even for a short time?

In my *head*,
during life's short run, I sometimes question Your ways.
But in my *heart*
I know that in the long run,
Your ways are always best.

Help me to listen to my *heart*
the next time all hell breaks lose!